Let's Measure Daylight

Organizing Data

I0811973

Sheri Lang

COMPUTER SCIENCE For the REAL World™

Rosen Classroom™

Published in 2018 by The Rosen Publishing Group, Inc.
29 East 21st Street, New York, NY 10010

Copyright © 2018 by The Rosen Publishing Group, Inc.

All rights reserved. No part of this book may be reproduced in any form without permission in writing from the publisher, except by a reviewer.

Book Design: Jennifer Ryder-Talbot
Editor: Caitie McAneney

Photo Credits: Cover Grisha Bruev/Shutterstock.com; p. 4 (daytime) Andrey Desfoto/Shutterstock.com; p. 4 (nighttime) Maxim Khytra/Shutterstock.com; p. 7 (earth) Alfonso de Tomas/Shutterstock.com; p. 8-9 emperorcosar/Shutterstock.com; p. 11 Africa Studio/Shutterstock.com; p. 12-13 Volodymyr Martyniuk/Shutterstock.com; p. 15 Rawpixel.com/Shutterstock.com; p. 20 everst/Shutterstock.com.

Library of Congress Cataloging-in-Publication Data

Names: Lang, Sheri.
Title: Let's measure daylight: organizing data / Sheri Lang.
Description: New York : Rosen Classroom, 2018. | Series: Computer Kids: Powered by Computational Thinking | Includes glossary and index.
Identifiers: LCCN ISBN 9781508137641 (pbk.) | ISBN 9781538324066 (library bound) | ISBN 9781538355473 (6 pack) | ISBN 9781508137375 (ebook)
Subjects: LCSH: Day--Juvenile literature. | Night--Juvenile literature. | Earth (Planet)--Rotation--Juvenile literature. | Graphic methods--Juvenile literature.
Classification: LCC QB633.L36 2018 | DDC 525'.35--dc23

Manufactured in the United States of America

CPSIA Compliance Information: Batch #WS18RC: For Further Information contact Rosen Publishing, New York, New York at 1-800-237-9932

Table of Contents

Day and Night

Have you ever watched a sunrise or a sunset? Have you ever stood outside when the sun was highest in the sky or when it was very dark out? You've seen the difference between daylight and nighttime firsthand.

Why does the sun seem to rise and fall in the sky? Is the sun moving or is Earth moving? The sun seems to rise and fall because Earth is rotating, or turning on its **axis**. The region where you live is facing the sun in the daylight. Earth moves so that your region is facing away from the sun at night. What kind of data might you collect about daylight?

Do you think the amount of daylight stays the same every day of the year? You can use data to find out!

How Long Is a Day?

You can collect data about the length of a day. First, you need to learn about seasons. The length of a day changes throughout different seasons at different locations on Earth. That's because Earth doesn't just rotate. It rotates on a tilted axis.

Earth's axis is like a rod that goes from top to bottom through the planet's center. At one time of the year, the Northern **Hemisphere** is tilted toward the sun. That's when the Northern Hemisphere has summer, which means longer days and hotter weather. At that same time, the Southern Hemisphere is tilted away from the sun. That's when the Southern Hemisphere has winter, which means shorter days and colder weather.

The Northern Hemisphere and Southern Hemisphere are separated by the equator. The equator is an imaginary line in between the two hemispheres.

Northern Hemisphere

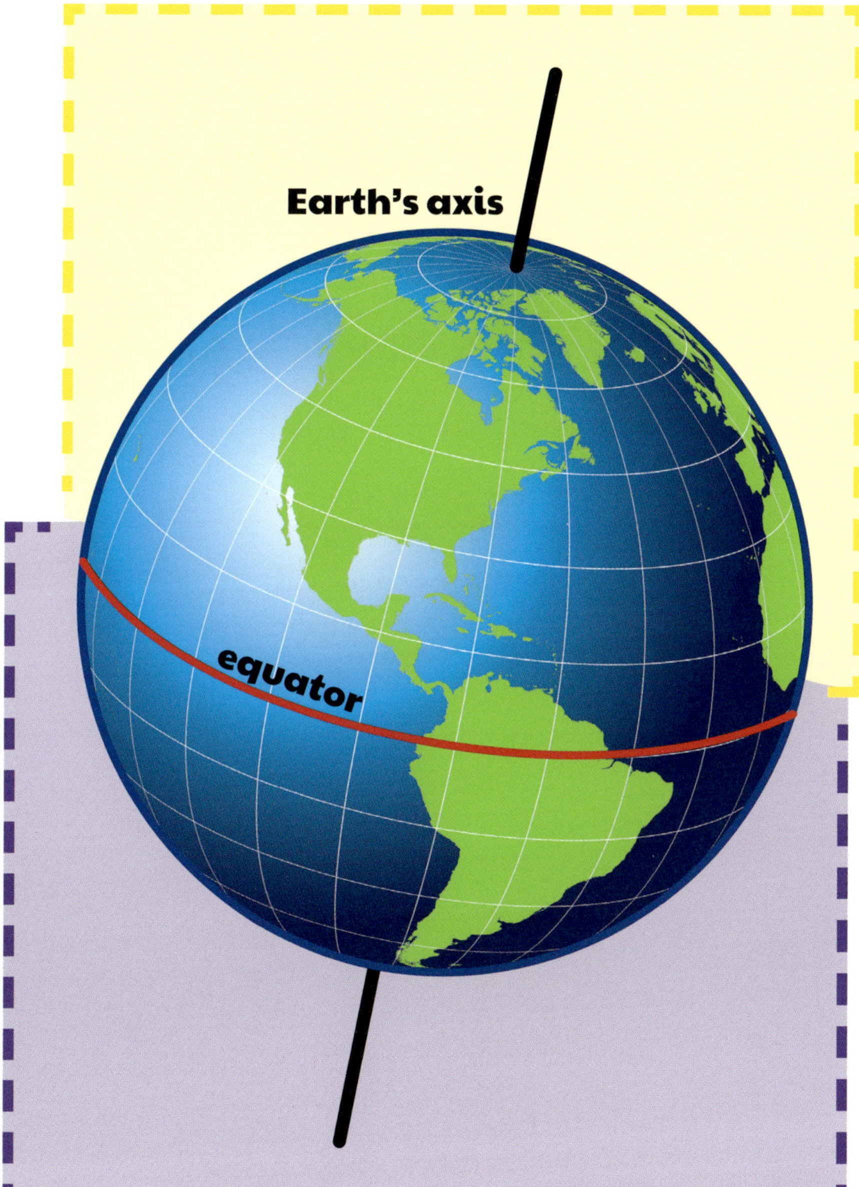

Southern Hemisphere

A Dramatic Shift

Some places have more **dramatic** shifts in the amount of daylight than others. For example, places along the equator don't have differing lengths of daylight throughout the year. That's because the equator is exactly halfway between the **poles**, so it doesn't matter which hemisphere is tilted towards the sun.

Alaska is part of the Arctic region. People who live there have to get used to nonstop sun in the summer!

The Arctic is a place where daylight shifts very dramatically throughout the year. This is the northernmost part of the Northern Hemisphere, close to the North Pole. In the winter, areas of the Arctic have darkness 24 hours every day. In the summer, areas of the Arctic have daylight 24 hours every day. That's quite a change for the people and animals living there!

Measuring Daylight

Now that you know about the way daylight changes through the year in different places on Earth, you can get started with data collection. First, choose your time span. Do you want to collect data for one week, one month, one season, or one year?

Imagine that you're going to collect data for a whole year. That will show you how the length of daylight changes from season to season. Let's assume that you live in the United States, which is in the Northern Hemisphere. In that case, you can guess that days will be longer in the summer than in the winter. Now, collect data to support that **hypothesis**!

Before you collect data, you might come up with a hypothesis for what you think you'll find.

Collecting Data

It may be best to start collecting data during a solstice. A solstice is one of two times a year when the sun reaches its highest or lowest point in the sky at noon. Solstices mark the longest and shortest days of the year. Imagine you start collecting data on the winter solstice for the Northern Hemisphere.

Each day, record the sunrise and sunset. You can get this information from the National Weather Service website. Then, do the math to find the amount of time between sunrise and sunset. For example, if the sun rises at 7 a.m. and sets at 8 p.m., then there were 13 hours of daylight that day.

If you track the motions of the sun, you'll see that it rises in the east and sets in the west.

Making a Bar Graph

If you collect data for the entire year, then you will have 365 numbers recorded to show the length of each day. That's a lot of data! You have to organize the data in order to analyze it more easily.

Charts and graphs are tools people use to organize data. They help people visualize, or picture, what the data means. They also help people spot trends in data. A bar graph has an **x-axis** and a **y-axis**. The y-axis depends on the x-axis. For your bar graph, you would have the 365 dates on the x-axis, or **horizontal** line. On the **vertical** y-axis, you would have the hours of daylight recorded on each day, from 0 to 24.

When there is a great amount of data, it is much easier to make your bar graph using online tools.

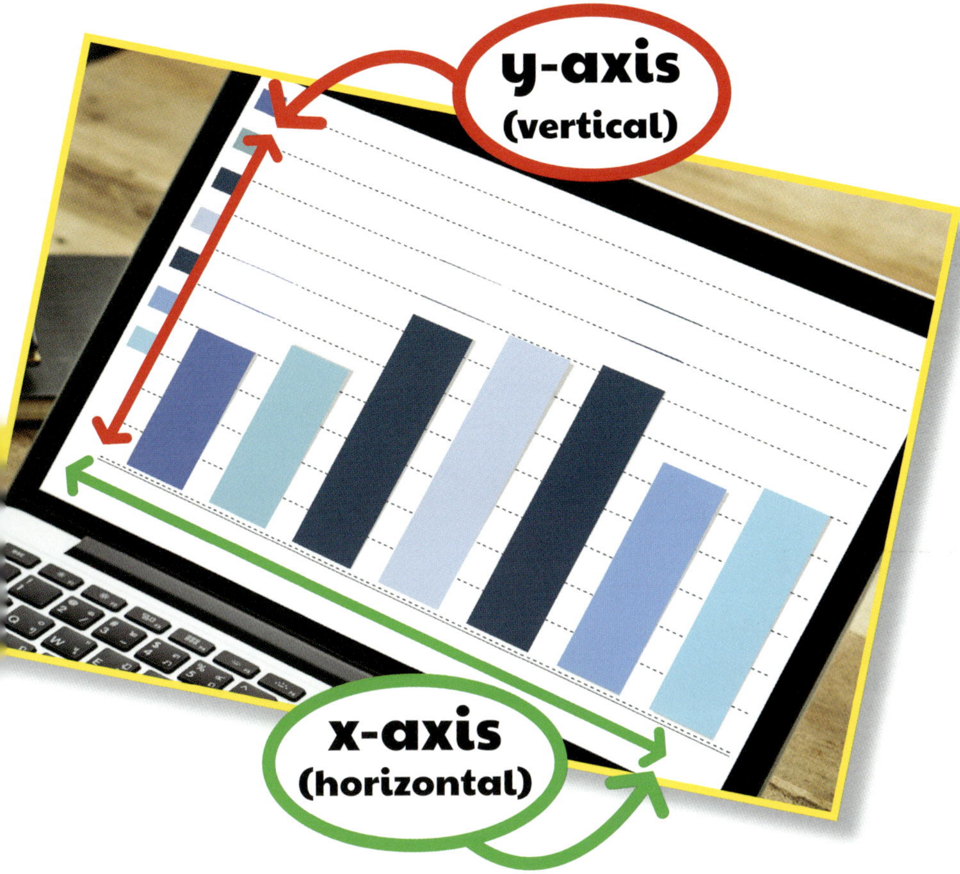

line graph

bar graph

Tools for Organizing Data

pie chart

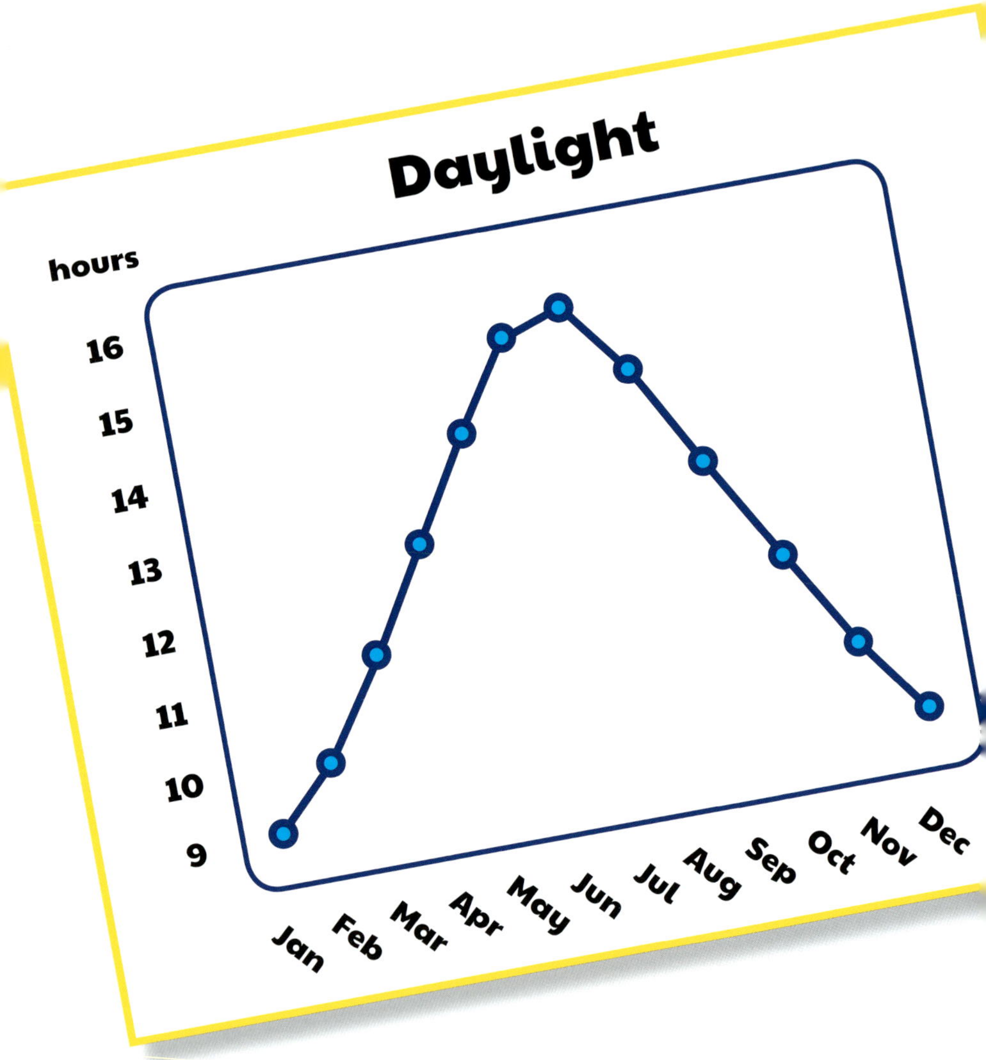
Daylight
hours
16
15
14
13
12
11
10
9
Jan
Feb
Mar
Apr
May
Jun
Jul
Aug
Sep
Oct
Nov
Dec

Making a Line Graph

You may have found that your bar graph was a bit cluttered with so many dates. Would a line graph be a better tool for organizing your data? Try it out!

Line graphs have an x-axis and y-axis just like a bar graph. However, you make a little dot where the x-axis value and y-axis value meet. Then, you connect the dots with a line. Like bar graphs, line graphs show trends. You can see that the line rises for half a year and then falls. That shows that after the winter solstice, the length of daylight increases until the summer solstice and then decreases again.

You could make a line graph with the length of daylight for the first day of each month. That will make graphing easier while still helping you visualize the pattern in the graph.

Making a Pie Chart

Pie charts are very different from bar graphs and line graphs. They aren't used to show how something changes over time. Instead, they are used to show how a whole thing is broken down into parts, like the pieces of a pie.

You can use a pie chart to show the part of each day that has daylight. For example, look for the day you recorded the most daylight. Imagine it was 15 hours on the summer solstice. You could use a pie chart to show that there was daylight for 15 hours out of 24 hours. Your pie chart would show you that there was much more daylight than darkness on that day.

This pie chart helps you visualize how much of a day is daylight and how much is nighttime.

Daylight

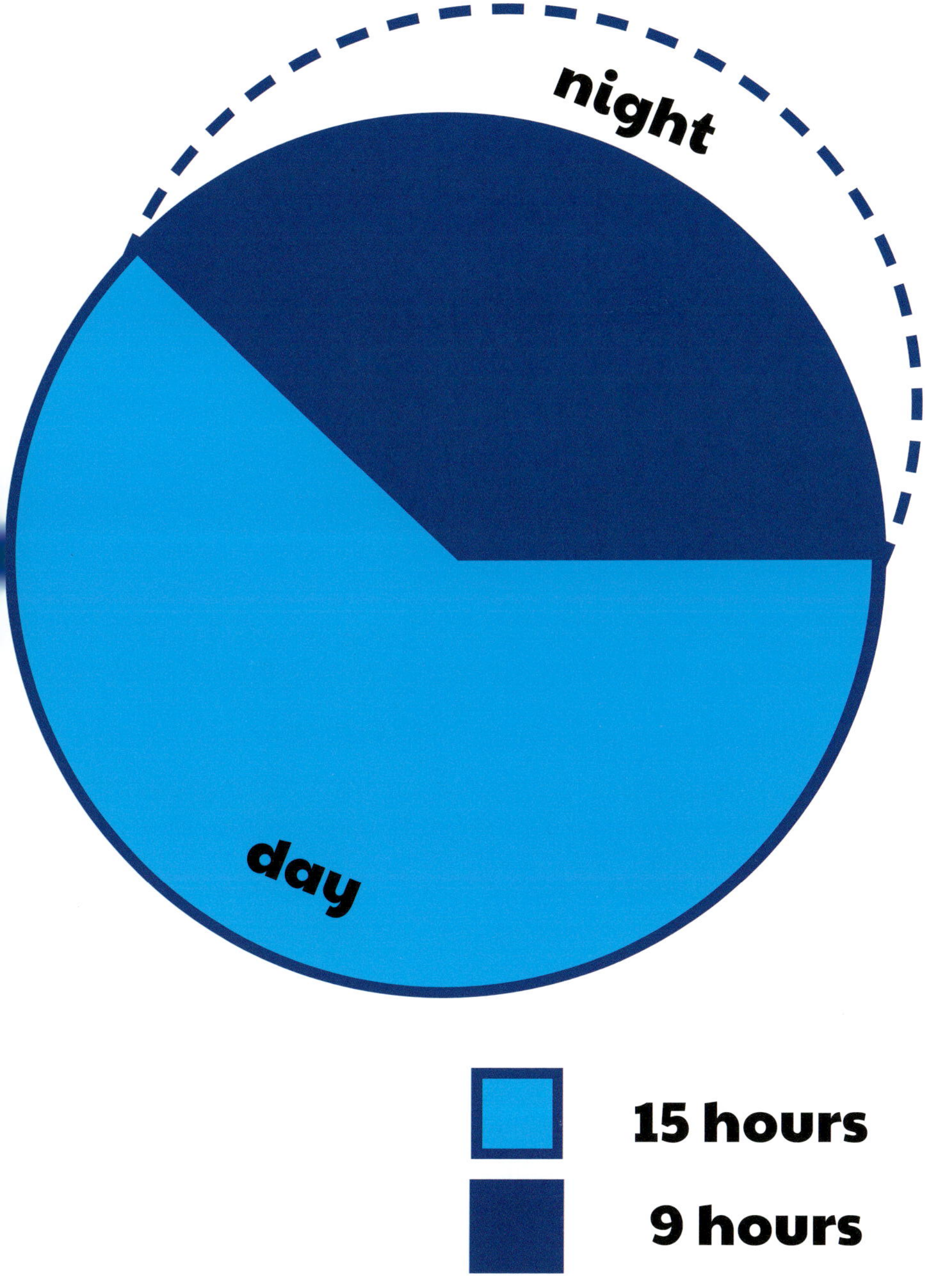

If there are only nine hours of daylight where you live this December, then you can predict that there will be the same amount next December.

What Do You See?

Once you've organized your data into graphs and charts, you can start to see patterns and trends. You may notice in your bar graph and line graph that there is a **gradual** increase until the summer solstice in June. Then then there is a gradual decrease until the winter solstice in December.

How can you use the data you've organized? You can use it to compare the length of daylight from one season to the next. Your data now supports the hypothesis that days are longer in the summer than in the winter. You can also use it to predict how much daylight there will be at a certain time of year in the future.

Let's Get Organized!

Collecting a large pool of data is a difficult task. Analyzing that amount of data can be even more difficult! One way to make this task easier is by organizing data into **accessible** graphs and charts. You can use the graphs and charts to help you compare values or even predict what might happen in the future.

Making a graph by hand on graph paper is possible, but it might take a while with so much data. Instead, you can use many computer tools to organize your data. You can make a graph using a computer program called Excel. You can also make a graph or chart using tools provided through educational websites.

Glossary

accessible: Capable of being used or understood.

axis: An imaginary straight line around which a planet turns.

dramatic: Sudden and extreme.

gradual: Changing or developing by small degrees at a time.

hemisphere: One-half of Earth.

horizontal: Level with the line that seems to form where the earth meets the sky.

hypothesis: An educated guess.

pole: Either end of the imaginary line on which Earth or another planet turns.

vertical: Straight up and down.

x-axis: The horizontal axis in a graph, which does not depend on the value of the y-axis.

y-axis: The vertical axis in the graph, which depends upon the value of the x-axis.

Index